Original title:
The Fellowship of Feelings

Copyright © 2024 Swan Charm
All rights reserved.

Author: Kätriin Kaldaru
ISBN HARDBACK: 978-9916-86-650-4
ISBN PAPERBACK: 978-9916-86-651-1
ISBN EBOOK: 978-9916-86-652-8

Constellations of Comfort

Under a blanket of stars, we lay,
Whispers of light guide our way.
In the silence, our hearts learn,
Finding solace as candles burn.

Memory dances with gentle grace,
Each twinkle reveals a familiar face.
In the vast skies above us bright,
We share our dreams, igniting the night.

Intertwined Journeys

Paths crossed in the softest glow,
Hand in hand, we wander slow.
Through valleys deep and mountains high,
Together we reach for the endless sky.

With each step, our stories blend,
Two hearts united, a journey to mend.
In laughter and tears, we'll write our tale,
A voyage unbroken, we shall not fail.

The Embrace of Understanding

In silence, we find words unspoken,
Hearts open wide, never broken.
With a glance, a bond is formed,
In shared moments, true love is warmed.

Gentle nods in the softest light,
We navigate shadows, holding tight.
In every sigh, insight appears,
An embrace that quiets our fears.

Moments of Mutuality

In the dance of give and take,
Each gesture nurtures, love awake.
We build a bridge, strong and true,
In every step, I walk with you.

A tapestry of shared delight,
Stitching dreams from day to night.
With every laugh, every tear,
In mutual moments, we find our cheer.

Mosaics of Sentiment

In fragments of joy, we find our way,
Colors of laughter, brightening the day.
Pieces of sorrow, woven with care,
Together they form a vibrant affair.

Whispers of love in the quiet night,
Echoes of hope in the morning light.
Each memory holds a story to tell,
In this grand mosaic, we weave our spell.

The tiles of our hearts, both rough and smooth,
Reflect the moments that help us to soothe.
Shattered and whole, we gather anew,
Crafting a landscape that's uniquely true.

Every emotion, a brushstroke bold,
In tales of our lives, all the shades unfold.
We're artists of spirit, creating our fate,
Mosaics of sentiment, wondrous and great.

United in beauty, together we stand,
In the gallery of life, hand in hand.
Through laughter and tears, we learn and we grow,
Mosaics of sentiment, ever aglow.

Choreography of Connection

In shadows we meet, where silence ignites,
With glances exchanged, we dance through the nights.
The rhythm of hearts, a pulse so refined,
In the choreography, our souls intertwined.

Step by step, with each gentle sway,
The language of touch invites us to play.
In moments of stillness, our spirits unite,
Creating a bond that feels just right.

Twirling through dreams, we rise and we fall,
Supporting each other, we conquer it all.
In the dance of our lives, no steps go to waste,
Every movement, a moment that life has embraced.

Together we move, a symphony pure,
With passion as fuel, we find our allure.
Through laughter and tears, in joy and in pain,
Choreography of connection, our own sweet refrain.

As seasons evolve, and we change with the tide,
Still anchored in love, we step side by side.
In this dance of existence, forever we flow,
Choreography of connection, binding us so.

Dance of Diverse Emotions

In the ballroom of life, we twirl with grace,
Emotions a tapestry, each stitch finds its place.
Joy leaps and spins with a radiant glow,
While sadness flows softly, as rivers below.

Anger ignites with a fierce, fiery storm,
Frustration insists on a shape yet to form.
Yet laughter erupts, a contagious release,
In the dance of our hearts, we find our peace.

Surprise takes a bow in extravagant hue,
Each feeling a partner, both old and new.
Together they weave a performance divine,
In the dance of emotions, all rhythms align.

Through valleys of doubt and mountains of trust,
Every step we take is an act we must.
In the theater of life, with roles yet to play,
We dance through the darkness and into the day.

Each twist and each turn, a lesson we learn,
In the dance of diverse emotions, we yearn.
Embracing the spectrum, we cherish the blend,
In this vivid performance, on love we depend.

Chronicles of Compassion

In the quiet whispers of a caring heart,
Lies the essence of love, a journey to start.
With hands reaching out to lighten the load,
Chronicles of compassion, a sacred road.

Every small gesture, a tender embrace,
Binding our spirits in this precious space.
Through kindness and grace, we rise and we mend,
Every chapter written, a message to send.

Holding each other through shadows and pain,
Finding our strength in the softest refrain.
Each story unfolds like petals in bloom,
In chronicles of compassion, we dispel the gloom.

With hearts wide open, we share in the plight,
For every lost soul, we turn on the light.
In acts of love, our spirits take flight,
We weave our connections, resilient and bright.

As pages keep turning, our tales intertwine,
In this shared narrative, compassion will shine.
Together we journey, our mission is clear,
In chronicles of compassion, we persevere.

Links of Laughter

In a room filled with smiles,
Echoes of joy resound,
Moments we cherish,
In laughter, we are found.

Whispers of humor light,
A spark in weary days,
Gathered around the fire,
In warmth, our heart sways.

Jokes pass like a breeze,
Bringing us close again,
In the dance of our mirth,
We forget all the pain.

With shared chuckles so bright,
Our spirits set free,
Ties woven in laughter,
Forever we'll be.

A tapestry of delight,
In each vibrant thread,
Linked through joyful moments,
Where happiness is spread.

Ties of Tender Understanding

In the silence we share,
A bond that runs deep,
Eyes meet in stillness,
Each secret we keep.

Words unspoken linger,
In gentle, knowing glances,
Hearts speak a language,
In the dance of our chances.

Through trials and triumphs,
Together we stand strong,
With kindness in our hearts,
Where we both belong.

In every soft gesture,
An embrace that heals,
In this tender understanding,
The truth reveals.

Bonds forged in patience,
With love as our guide,
In the warmth of connection,
Our hearts open wide.

Fireflies of Fellowship

Under the stars that twinkle,
Friendship lights the night,
With fireflies dancing,
In the soft, silver light.

Together we wander,
In the calm of the breeze,
Our laughter igniting,
Like whispers through trees.

Moments like lanterns,
In a world of our own,
Guiding us gently,
With love as our throne.

We gather these memories,
Like dreams in our hands,
In the glow of connection,
We make our own plans.

So here's to the evenings,
And the bonds that we build,
In the magic of fellowship,
Our hearts forever thrilled.

Affirmations of Affection

In every warm embrace,
Love whispers our name,
With each gentle touch,
A burning, bright flame.

Words like soft petals,
Fall lightly like rain,
In the garden of trust,
Where we both remain.

Each glance like sunshine,
Warming up the soul,
In the dance of our hearts,
We become whole.

A tapestry of feelings,
Woven thread by thread,
In the space of our laughter,
And all that is said.

So here's to the moments,
Where love's light shines bright,
In the affirmations of truth,
Our hearts take flight.

Gifts of Gratitude

In morning's light, a smile shines bright,
Thankful hearts lift spirits high.
Each small gesture, a pure delight,
Echoes of love, never shy.

With whispers soft, we share our thanks,
For kindness shown, for laughter shared.
Through gentle ways, our joy expands,
In bonds of warmth, we are ensnared.

A simple note, a thoughtful prayer,
In twilight's glow, we pause to see.
These gifts of grace, beyond compare,
Remind us of our unity.

In every heart, a seed is sown,
A garden rich with trust and care.
Through storms of life, we've grown and grown,
Together always, a love we share.

So let us weave this tapestry,
Of gratitude in every thread.
With open hearts, we'll always be,
In harmony, where love is spread.

Lullabies of Loyalty

Under the stars, our promises lie,
In whispered dreams, our vows are tight.
With every dawn, our spirits fly,
Bonded by truths that feel so right.

Through trials faced and paths we tread,
Loyalty blooms, steadfast and bold.
In tender words, our hearts are fed,
Stories of love eternally told.

With every heartbeat, a song we weave,
A melody strong, a steadfast theme.
Through darkest nights, we won't deceive,
In loyal hearts, we find our dream.

Amidst the chaos, through thick and thin,
Together we stand, never apart.
With every breath, a life to begin,
In loyalty's grip, we guard our heart.

So hush your worries and rest your soul,
In gentle arms, find peace tonight.
With lullabies that make us whole,
We embrace the dawn with hearts alight.

Harmonizing Hearts

In a symphony of gentle sighs,
Our hearts align, a sweet embrace.
With every note, our spirits rise,
Creating space in love's warm grace.

Together we dance, a rhythm found,
In steps that echo through the night.
With laughter's tune, we spin around,
In harmony, we find our light.

Through trials faced, we blend our song,
With voices strong, we rise above.
In every chord, we belong,
Where melodies bind our trust and love.

As seasons change, our tune remains,
A chorus of hope that never fades.
With open hearts, we break the chains,
In unity, our joy cascades.

So let the music fill the air,
In every heartbeat, let it flow.
In this sweet space, beyond compare,
With harmonizing hearts, we grow.

Shadows of Shared Light

In twilight's glow, shadows might linger,
Yet light, it dances in the dark.
With every touch, we spark a finger,
Illuminating paths, a spark.

Through storms we stand, side by side,
Each challenge faced, a tale of fight.
Together we turn the tide,
Creating joy from shared insight.

In moments rare, we catch a glimmer,
Reflections bright in love's embrace.
Though shadows fall, our hope grows slimmer,
For hand in hand, we find our place.

As dawn breaks new, with colors bold,
Our shadows merge in morning's light.
With stories shared, our hearts unfold,
In unity, we shine so bright.

So let us walk this path with grace,
Through every shadow we may find.
In shared light's glow, we find our space,
Together, hearts forever intertwined.

Weaving this Fabric of Emotions

Threads of joy entwine with sorrow,
Each stitch a tale of tomorrow.
Colors clash, yet they harmonize,
In this tapestry, love never lies.

We gather moments, both sharp and sweet,
In the warmth of memories, we meet.
Every fold holds a hidden truth,
Whispers of wisdom, the heart's youth.

Stitches echo in laughter and tears,
Woven through hopes, silencing fears.
This fabric holds all the dreams we weave,
In its embrace, we learn to believe.

Patterns emerge from the rhythm of days,
Sunset and dawn in intricate ways.
The loom of life spins bright and dim,
Yet through it all, we dance in hymn.

With each knot, a story we tell,
Threads binding tightly, weaving so well.
In this tale of emotions, a rich array,
We find our strength, come what may.

Fusion of Fragments

Scattered pieces, lost and found,
In chaos, beauty can abound.
Each shard reflects a story's start,
A mosaic formed from the heart.

Colors clash, yet find their place,
In this dance, we learn to embrace.
From fragments, new patterns emerge,
A symphony of voices converge.

Broken dreams turn to hopeful skies,
In every fracture, a chance to rise.
Threads of the past weave tight and fast,
In the now, we find peace at last.

Together we mend, together we grow,
In the garden of life, love's seeds we sow.
Each fragment a note in the song we sing,
In harmony, we find the joy we bring.

Through the lens of our shared embrace,
We redefine what holds us in grace.
A fusion of fragments, strong and bright,
Creating magic in the darkest night.

Radiant Tides of Togetherness

Waves of warmth roll in from the sea,
The tide of love pulls you close to me.
In the ebb and flow, we find our way,
Radiant dreams carry us each day.

Under the moon's soft, guiding light,
We gather strength, we shine so bright.
Each heartbeat a rhythm, a dance in time,
Together we soar, in perfect rhyme.

The ocean whispers secrets, so profound,
In its embrace, our hopes are found.
Tides of trust lift us ever high,
Together, we can reach the sky.

Through storms that threaten to pull apart,
We hold on tightly, heart to heart.
In the stillness, we find our peace,
Radiant tides that never cease.

Through shifting sands and changing skies,
In togetherness, true love lies.
Each wave a promise, a pledge made new,
In this ocean of hearts, it's me and you.

Bridges Across the Heart

Spanning the chasms of doubt and fear,
A bridge of trust emerges here.
With each step, we break the divide,
Together we stand, hearts open wide.

Built from kindness, crafted with care,
Each beam a testament, strong and rare.
In the winds of change, we hold so fast,
These bonds of love, forever will last.

Every crossing, a journey begun,
Through sunshine and storms, we overcome.
On this path, we share our dreams,
Building a future, or so it seems.

Hand in hand, we traverse the way,
With laughter and hope, brightening the gray.
Each bridge we build draws us near,
Creating a path that knows no fear.

So let's cherish these spans we create,
Bridges of love that conquer fate.
In every heartbeat, in every part,
We find our courage, bridges across the heart.

Tides of Togetherness

The ocean whispers, soft and clear,
With every wave, you draw me near.
Together we walk on shifting sand,
Building a world, just you and I stand.

As tides embrace the moonlit shore,
Our hearts align, forevermore.
In the ebb and flow, we find our place,
Two souls entwined in timeless grace.

The sun sets low, painting the sky,
In every shade, our dreams rely.
With laughter shared and tears released,
In love's sweet tide, we are at peace.

As seasons change, we weather storms,
In every twist, our bond transforms.
Hand in hand, we face the fight,
Finding joy in every night.

Through trials faced and treasures sought,
It's you, my love, who holds my thought.
Together we rise, together we shine,
In the tides of love, forever divine.

Conversations in Color

In whispers soft, we share our dreams,
Painting the world in vibrant streams.
Each color speaks in tones so bright,
Illuminating shadows, merging light.

With every stroke, your laughter flows,
A canvas rich, where friendship grows.
Blues of calm and reds of fire,
In every hue, our souls conspire.

The greens of hope brush gently near,
While yellows dance, erasing fear.
Together we blend, a masterpiece,
In this gallery, hearts find peace.

As tones entwine, in vibrant grace,
We craft a world, our sacred space.
Through every shade, in tethered trust,
In colorful talks, we find what's just.

The palette shifts, but still we stay,
In conversations, we find our way.
A spectrum rich, forever we'll roam,
In artful words, we build our home.

Driftwood of Deep Bonds

Amidst the waves, the driftwood lies,
Stories whispered through timeless skies.
Each knot and grain, a tale retold,
Of friendships forged, of love so bold.

With every tide, we wash ashore,
Carrying memories we both adore.
In the strength of wood, our lives align,
Bound together, our fates entwined.

The currents shift, yet still we cling,
To pieces of hope that nature brings.
Through storms endured, we stand as one,
In the dance of life, we've just begun.

The ocean's breath, a serenade,
In the gentle waves, our fears will fade.
Driftwood's strength, a loving guide,
In deepening bonds, we take our stride.

As the sun sets and shadows play,
We cherish the driftwood, come what may.
Through ebb and flow, our spirits soar,
In united hearts, we find our shore.

Palette of Shared Dreams

In twilight hues, we paint our hopes,
A canvas stretched across the sky.
With strokes of laughter, love elopes,
Together, we let our spirits fly.

Each color whispers tales untold,
Of journeys marked by paths we've shared.
In unity, our hearts unfold,
A tapestry of dreams prepared.

With every brush, we blend the light,
Creating visions strong and bright.
In every shade, a world ignites,
Together, we can take to flight.

Through storms and sun, through chill and heat,
Our palette speaks of bonds so deep.
With every heartbeat, we compete,
In shared dreams, our memories keep.

So let us mix our colors vast,
In unity, we'll always last.

Constellations of Care

Above us shine the stars so bright,
Each one a promise, soft and near.
In darkness flows the gentle light,
A reminder that you are here.

With twinkling eyes and whispered prayers,
We weave our hearts through night's embrace.
In every challenge, love prepares,
A constellation, a sacred place.

Through trials faced, the paths we tread,
The bonds of care will guide us home.
In every tear that's gently shed,
We find the strength to rise and roam.

With every moment shared in time,
We sketch the skies in hues so rare.
In quiet awe, our hearts will rhyme,
A celestial dance of tender care.

So let us reach, our hands entwined,
In this vast universe we find.

Resounding Resonance

In echoes strong, our voices call,
A symphony of hearts in tune.
Through valleys deep and mountains tall,
Together, we can face the moon.

With every note, a story grows,
In harmony, our spirits soar.
The rhythm speaks of love that flows,
A melody we can't ignore.

In every silence, a refrain,
Resounding gently through the air.
A bond unbroken, never vain,
With trust, we rise beyond despair.

So let the music guide our way,
In waves that crash, in stillness found.
In every heartbeat, night and day,
We'll find the chain that keeps us bound.

Our song, a treasure to embrace,
Resounding whispers through the space.

Embrace of Empathy

In hushed moments, we draw near,
With open hearts and listening ears.
Through tender glances, we can see,
The beauty in raw honesty.

With gentle words, we weave our tales,
A fabric rich with every thread.
In shared struggles, love prevails,
A soft embrace where fears can shed.

Through storms we find the calm within,
In every hug, a healing balm.
With every push, we shed the skin,
Of loneliness, we find the calm.

In empathy, our spirits dance,
A rhythm steady, a warm embrace.
In understanding, we find chance,
To bridge the gaps, to make our place.

So let us hold, with arms so wide,
The world we share, our hearts collide.

Tides of Togetherness

In the ebb and flow we find,
Hearts entwined in gentle binds.
Waves of laughter crash and rise,
A dance beneath the vast blue skies.

Moments shared like grains of sand,
Softly slipping through our hands.
Yet each tide that pulls away,
Bears memories that forever stay.

Together, we face what comes at dawn,
Each challenge met, we carry on.
In harmony, our spirits glide,
In the sea of love, we take our ride.

With every whisper of the breeze,
We find comfort, hearts at ease.
In tides of joy or sorrow's song,
In togetherness, we all belong.

So let us walk the shoreline clear,
With steadfast trust, we draw near.
In this ocean, vast and bright,
Our bond shines like the stars at night.

The Quilt of Interactions

Stitched together, thread by thread,
Each moment shared, a memory spread.
In colors bright, our stories weave,
A tapestry of hearts that believe.

Laughter echoes through the squares,
Comfort found in all our cares.
In each patch, a tale untold,
The warmth of friendship, pure as gold.

Through tears and joy, the quilt expands,
Embracing all with open hands.
A shelter soft in storms we face,
A woven sky of love and grace.

Every square a life displayed,
In patterns of the bonds we've made.
Together, strong against the fray,
A quilt of interactions here to stay.

So let us cherish every seam,
The threads of purpose, hope, and dream.
In our quilt, we find our home,
In love's embrace, we're never alone.

Lighthouses in the Storm

Amidst the darkness, shines a light,
Guiding souls through the night.
With every flash, a beacon's song,
Reminding us that we are strong.

In tempests fierce, we stand our ground,
The lighthouse helps, our hearts are found.
Through turbulent waves, it carries hope,
In shadowed moments, it helps us cope.

The storm may rage, the winds may wail,
But together we will set our sail.
In unison, we brave the fear,
A lighthouse shines, forever near.

With every storm that comes our way,
We find our strength, we will not sway.
In the heart of chaos, love will bloom,
Guiding us through the darkest gloom.

So in the storm, remember this:
A light will shine, a gentle kiss.
Together, we are never lost,
For lighthouses guide, no matter the cost.

Landscapes of Shared Experience

In valleys deep and mountains high,
We walk together, you and I.
Through winding paths and rivers wide,
In shared experiences, we abide.

The colors bloom in vibrant hues,
With every choice, a story dues.
In nature's arms, we learn and grow,
In landscapes vast, our spirits flow.

Moments captured in the breeze,
Embracing life with joyful ease.
Through ups and downs, we'll always find,
The beauty of the ties that bind.

Each sunset paints a brand new start,
Together holding every heart.
In whispered thoughts and laughter's song,
We share a world where we belong.

So let us wander, hand in hand,
Exploring all this life has planned.
In landscapes rich with love's embrace,
Together we'll find our perfect place.

Threads of Kinship

In the tapestry of life, we weave,
Connections form, hearts believe.
Every thread, a story spun,
Through laughter shared, two become one.

Through trials faced, and joys we find,
The ties that hold us, deeply bind.
In whispered secrets, trust is born,
Through seasons change, our love's not worn.

From different paths, we journey on,
These threads of kinship, never gone.
In warmth of arms, or gentle sighs,
Together we'll rise, under vast skies.

Our lineage blooms, its roots run deep,
In memories cherished, we softly keep.
Through every joy, and every sorrow,
We craft a bond that shapes tomorrow.

So here we stand, hand in hand,
In this tapestry, together we stand.
With threads of kinship, strong and bright,
We paint our love, a beacon of light.

Celestial Ties of Emotion

Beneath the stars, our spirits soar,
Celestial ties that bind us more.
With every heartbeat, every glance,
In cosmos vast, we find our dance.

The moonlight whispers, soft and clear,
In shadows cast, I feel you near.
With constellations guiding our way,
We chase the night, till break of day.

In depths of space, our souls align,
Together woven, fate divine.
Through galaxies, our love will thrive,
In stardust dreams, we come alive.

A comet's tail, our passion's flight,
Exploring realms of endless night.
These ties of emotion, a brilliant glow,
In all the universe, we surely know.

So let us wander, hand in hand,
Amongst the stars, a timeless band.
With celestial ties that never fade,
In love's embrace, we are remade.

The Dance of Heartfelt Bonds

In rhythm found, our hearts entwine,
A dance of love, so pure, divine.
With laughter spun, the music plays,
We sway together, through life's maze.

Each step we take, with grace and flair,
In heartfelt bonds, we breathe the air.
A twirl of joy, a dip of trust,
In every moment, it's a must.

Through shared dreams, and whispered hopes,
A journey paved, with loving ropes.
In this embrace, our spirits blend,
The dance of bonds that never end.

With every beat, our souls connect,
In passion's rhythm, we reflect.
As twilight falls, we take the floor,
In heartfelt dance, we crave for more.

So let the music play its tune,
Beneath the stars, the silver moon.
In dance of bonds, we find our place,
Forever bound in love's sweet grace.

Intersections of Intimacy

At the crossroads where two hearts meet,
Intersections of intimacy, bittersweet.
In silent glances, unspoken words,
Our souls entwined, like flight of birds.

In shared spaces, both near and far,
We navigate, like guiding stars.
Through every challenge, we find our way,
In the warmth of love, come what may.

With tender moments, our spirits blend,
In every heartbeat, we comprehend.
As pathways cross, we boldly tread,
Together charting where hopes are spread.

In laughter shared, or tears we weep,
These intersections, our secrets keep.
Through winding roads, we forge anew,
In intimacy, I find you true.

So here we stand, at life's grand gate,
In quiet corners, we contemplate.
In intersections, love's journey starts,
A dance of intimacy, two beating hearts.

Canvas of Collective Heartbeats

In the whispers of the night,
We paint dreams with soft light.
Each heartbeat a stroke divine,
Together we create, align.

Colors blend in harmony,
Our fears fade, we're wild and free.
United, our spirits soar high,
In this canvas, we won't shy.

Our laughter echoes like art,
Creating beauty from the heart.
Every moment, we embrace,
In each other's warm space.

Threads of joy that intertwine,
In silence, our souls combine.
Every heartbeat matters here,
In our union, we persevere.

With every brush of kindness,
We break free from the darkness.
A tapestry of our song,
In this canvas, we belong.

Melodies of Mutual Support

With every note, we carry grace,
Lifting up this sacred space.
Harmonies that intertwine,
Build a bridge, hearts align.

In the chorus, we stand tall,
Every whisper, a clarion call.
Together, we sing our truth,
Cherishing the dreams of youth.

In this symphony we play,
Melodies will light the way.
Notes of hope in every line,
Bound together, we will shine.

When shadows begin to creep,
In each other's arms, we leap.
With the rhythm, we find strength,
United, we'll go any length.

Voices rise like morning sun,
In this journey, we are one.
Every heart, a beat divine,
In the music, we will shine.

Connections that Breathe

In the spaces in between,
Connections spark, unseen, serene.
With each breath, a bond we weave,
In this embrace, we dare believe.

Gentle words, like softest air,
Fill our lungs, dispel despair.
With every sigh, a story told,
In our hearts, a warmth to hold.

Roots entwined beneath the ground,
In togetherness, we are found.
Nurtured by the love we share,
In this life, we breathe, we care.

Through the trials and the strife,
Connections breathe, we feel alive.
With every heartbeat, we renew,
In this journey, me and you.

As the seasons shift and change,
Our ties grow deep, rearrange.
In this dance, the rhythm flows,
Together, our garden grows.

Vows of Vulnerability

In the quiet, we unfold,
Vows of truth, precious as gold.
With open hearts, we share our fears,
In every tear, beauty appears.

Words unguarded, souls laid bare,
In each moment, love to share.
Together, we brave the night,
In our weakness, find the light.

Admitting what we often hide,
In this space, we will confide.
With every vow, we take a stand,
Together, hand in hand.

Lessons learned through pain and grace,
A sacred time, a cherished place.
In our hearts, we build a home,
In vulnerability, we roam.

As the world may seem unkind,
In each other, strength we find.
With every promise, every tear,
Vows of love, forever clear.

Gathering of Hearts

In a field where dreams ignite,
Fellow souls come into sight.
Together in laughter, they unite,
A tapestry of warmth and light.

Echoes of stories softly shared,
In moments sweet, souls are bared.
Through trials faced and burdens shared,
A bond is formed, compassion squared.

Time stands still in gentle grace,
Every smile a warm embrace.
In this haven, there's no race,
Just love's rhythm, a steady pace.

Hearts entwined, a whispered song,
In this space, we all belong.
Together, we are always strong,
A gathering where love is throng.

As dusk falls, we light the flame,
Each heart a glow, none the same.
In unity, we speak our name,
A gathering of love's acclaim.

Chorus of Compassion

Softly in the quiet night,
Voices rise, a shared delight.
In harmony, we find our might,
A chorus born from hearts alight.

Gentle hands extend with care,
Bridging gaps, a bond we share.
Caring hearts, a love laid bare,
In every note, hope fills the air.

Through sorrow's song, we draw near,
Kindness wraps us, oh so dear.
With every pulse, we persevere,
A chorus strong, we calm the fear.

In the echoes, we create,
Moments fleeting, but oh so great.
Together, love we cultivate,
This chorus, a united fate.

Hand in hand, we share the tune,
Underneath the silver moon.
In compassion, our spirits swoon,
A song that makes the darkness prune.

Mosaic of Moods

Colors blend and stories weave,
Each emotion we perceive.
In this art, we can believe,
A mosaic that helps us grieve.

In the laughter, bright and bold,
Soft sadness in shades of gold.
Every hue a tale retold,
Together, we are manifold.

Moments capture pain and light,
In the chaos, we take flight.
Like stars that twinkle in the night,
Our moods dance in pure delight.

With every brushstroke, lives collide,
A gallery where tears abide.
In unity, hearts open wide,
A mosaic that can't divide.

In this space, we find our place,
Embracing each and every face.
In the blend, a warm embrace,
A masterpiece of love's grace.

Dance of Diverse Emotions

In twilight's glow, the dancers meet,
A rhythm found beneath their feet.
With every beat, the heart skips fleet,
A celebration, life's heartbeat.

Joy spins round with vibrant flair,
While sorrow's shadow lingers there.
In every step, we breathe the air,
A dance made whole, because we care.

Anger leaps with fierce intent,
While calmness flows, a soft lament.
In this space, each mood is meant,
A dance of life, our hearts consent.

Hope waltzes gently through the fray,
In the blend, we find our way.
With every pirouette and sway,
Diverse emotions start to play.

Underneath the starry sky,
We spin and twirl, let spirits fly.
In this dance, we personify,
The beautiful truth that we all rely.

Intersections of Intimacy

At twilight's edge, we often meet,
In whispered words, our hearts repeat.
The space between feels warm and small,
In every glance, we lose our fall.

Fragments of dreams, we gently weave,
The trust we share, a silent reprieve.
Starlit paths that guide our way,
In tender moments, night turns to day.

Your laughter lingers in the air,
A melody that strokes the fair.
In the embrace of fragile light,
Our souls entwined, we take our flight.

With every step, our shadows blend,
In each heartbeat, love will mend.
Through all the fears, we bravely stand,
Together always, hand in hand.

As seasons shift, our bond blooms bright,
In every challenge, find the light.
Among the stars, we write our song,
In intersections, we belong.

Sonnet of Shared Sorrows

Upon the canvas, shadows fall,
Each brushstroke marks a silent call.
In sorrow's grip, we grasp our fate,
A symphony of hearts that wait.

In whispered secrets, wounds unfold,
The warmth of hands, a tale retold.
Through tempest skies, we learn to sail,
In unity, we cannot fail.

When quiet tears begin to flow,
In shared embrace, we start to grow.
A bond that's forged in trials deep,
Together, every promise we keep.

In moments dark, your light will shine,
Through every storm, your heart is mine.
As dawn ascends, we face the day,
In shared sorrows, we find our way.

Together strong, we rise anew,
A tapestry of shades and hue.
In every heartbeat, we will thrive,
Through shared sorrows, we survive.

Tapestry of Trust

In threads of gold, our lives entwine,
A tapestry that you and I design.
Each promise knit, each story told,
In every fold, our hearts behold.

As seasons shift, the colors blend,
In every tear, our values mend.
With every stitch, a scene unfolds,
In warmth and love, our bond upholds.

Through trials faced, we rise again,
Together woven, joy and pain.
In patterns rich, our journeys flow,
In trust, a radiant warmth will grow.

As laughter echoes in the night,
With woven hearts, we embrace the light.
Each thread a heartbeat, strong and true,
In this tapestry, there's me and you.

A legacy of dreams we chase,
In every curve, we find our place.
Through life's design, we stand as one,
In this tapestry, we've just begun.

Paths of Profound Understanding

Upon this road, we walk as one,
In every step, our fears are spun.
Through fields of doubt, we find our way,
Together strong, we seize the day.

With open hearts, we learn to see,
The beauty in our shared decree.
In quiet moments, truths unfold,
In understanding, we break the mold.

As rivers flow, our thoughts converge,
In harmony, our dreams emerge.
Through stormy nights, we gather light,
Our paths entwined, forever bright.

With every question, answers bloom,
In every shadow, we find room.
Together, we create our lore,
In paths profound, we seek for more.

As dawn unfolds, we journey on,
In every step, a new refrain.
Through life's wild roads, hand in hand,
In trust and love, forever stand.

Bonds Beyond Words

In silence we find strength,
A glance speaks a truth,
Our hearts dance together,
In joy and in youth.

Through storms and through trials,
Together we stand tall,
No words need be spoken,
Our love conquers all.

Shared laughter and tears,
Each moment we embrace,
In the stillness we cherish,
Our own sacred space.

The whispers of friendship,
A touch soft and kind,
In the depths of our bond,
True solace we find.

In this life's fleeting journey,
We weave our own thread,
With bonds beyond words,
In hearts we are led.

Cadence of Compassion

A gentle heartbeat echoes,
In every soul we meet,
With kindness we will flourish,
Through each act, so sweet.

In shadows, we offer light,
A hand held out in grace,
Together we'll uplift,
In this vast, shared space.

The whispers of kindness,
Resound in the night air,
With each step in compassion,
We show others we care.

In the rhythm of our giving,
We dance to a soft song,
With hearts intertwined,
Together we belong.

For every tear that's fallen,
We offer a warm embrace,
In the cadence of compassion,
Love finds its perfect place.

Symphony of Souls

Each note tells a story,
In harmony we blend,
With every breath we take,
Our spirits transcend.

Through laughter and through sorrow,
Together we will play,
In the symphony of life,
In night and in day.

With melodies of friendship,
We rise and we fall,
In the grand composition,
There's beauty in all.

The whispers of connection,
Resonate so clear,
In the music of our souls,
Love is always near.

As we compose this journey,
With grace, we unfold,
In the symphony of souls,
Our stories are told.

Threads of Togetherness

With every thread we weave,
A tapestry of dreams,
Together we create,
Our love softly gleams.

In the fabric of our lives,
Each moment's a stitch,
Through laughter and through pain,
We find our bright niche.

The colors may vary,
Yet vibrant, they show,
In the threads of togetherness,
We flourish and grow.

With hands joined in unity,
We face what may come,
In this beautiful journey,
Together we're one.

For each thread that connects us,
Is a bond that won't break,
In the fabric of life,
Together we make.

Whirlwind of Warm Feelings

In gentle breeze, hearts sway and dance,
A flicker of warmth, a fleeting chance.
Like petals that whisper in the sun,
Each moment shared, a joy begun.

A soft embrace, a knowing glance,
In tender silence, we take our stance.
The laughter rises, a sweet refrain,
In every heartbeat, love's gentle gain.

Through stormy skies, we find our way,
With hands entwined, we'll never stray.
A pathway forged of dreams and care,
In this whirlwind, we always share.

Like ripples on water, feelings spread,
In every word, a truth unsaid.
Through trials faced, we will hold tight,
In this whirlwind, we find our light.

So here we stand, our spirits high,
Beneath the vast and endless sky.
Together we rise, with courage bold,
In this whirlwind, our hearts unfold.

Voices in Vivid Unity

A chorus of souls, harmonies blend,
In vibrant colors, our hearts ascend.
Each note a story, a woven thread,
In this unity, no words are left unsaid.

Through laughter and tears, we walk as one,
Under the moon and the blazing sun.
Together we rise, hand in hand,
In this vivid world, together we stand.

Like rivers flowing, our voices combine,
In the garden of dreams, our spirits shine.
Echoes of kindness, resonant sound,
In the dance of life, our joys abound.

With every heartbeat, a promise is made,
In the canvas of time, our love displayed.
Through trials and storms, we shall not break,
In vivid unity, our souls awake.

So here we sing, with passion and grace,
In the tapestry woven, we find our place.
Together we dream, through shadows and light,
Voices in unity, shining so bright.

Kaleidoscope of Kindness

In swirling colors, kindness appears,
Softening edges, calming our fears.
Each act a prism, refracting light,
In the kaleidoscope, hearts take flight.

With gentle words, we nurture hope,
Through kindness shared, we learn to cope.
A smile exchanged, a hand to lend,
In this world, we become a friend.

Like threads of gold in a tapestry,
We weave our stories, you and me.
Each moment cherished, a love profound,
In the kaleidoscope, beauty is found.

From simple gestures, a bond can grow,
In the garden of kindness, seeds we sow.
Through every challenge, we hold the key,
In this vibrant dance, we are free.

So let us shine, our hearts ablaze,
In the kaleidoscope, we find our ways.
Together we rise, like flowers in bloom,
In kindness shared, let love consume.

Bubbles of Blissful Bonds

In bubbles of laughter, joy takes flight,
Floating on dreams, in pure delight.
Each moment shared, a treasure rare,
In this bond, we find love's care.

With every pop, new memories form,
In the warmth of friendship, we weather the storm.
Through playful whispers, secrets exchanged,
In bubbles of bliss, hearts are rearranged.

Like waves on the shore, our laughter rings,
In the dance of life, we embrace all things.
With every smile, a spark ignites,
In this bubble, our spirits take flight.

Through shimmering light, we navigate time,
In gentle moments, life's sweet rhyme.
With every heartbeat, we are entwined,
In bubbles of bliss, joy we find.

So let us soar, like bubbles in air,
In our blissful bonds, love's magic we share.
Together we dream, on this hopeful ride,
In the realm of our hearts, forever allied.

Reflections in a Shared Mirror

In the glass, we see our dreams,
Dancing light in soft moonbeams.
A glimpse of laughter, a flicker of pain,
In this mirror, we search again.

Your eyes hold stories yet untold,
A warmth within, a heart of gold.
Together we weave a tapestry bright,
In reflections, we find our light.

Waves of thoughts, gentle yet strong,
The whispered truths where we belong.
Together we stand, hand in hand,
In this mirrored world, we understand.

Shadows linger, yet hope remains,
In laughter's echo, love refrains.
Through the trials and the tears we see,
A shared journey, you and me.

As the dawn breaks, we embrace the day,
Reflections guide us, come what may.
In the shared mirror, we find our way,
Together forever, come what may.

Whispers of the Heart

In the silence, secrets flow,
Whispered dreams that softly glow.
A touch, a glance, a knowing smile,
In these whispers, we walk a mile.

Echoes linger in twilight's grace,
Soft reminders of love's embrace.
Each heartbeat sings a silent song,
In the whispers where we belong.

Tender moments, fleeting yet pure,
In every sigh, we find our cure.
Connected souls, a sacred bond,
In whispered words, we rise beyond.

The heart speaks truth without a sound,
In its rhythm, our trust is found.
With every whisper, dreams take flight,
Guided gently by love's light.

As the night unfolds its gentle art,
We listen closely, whispers of the heart.
Together we thrive in this tender space,
In the softness of whispers, we find our place.

Tapestry of Emotions

Threads of joy, strands of sorrow,
Woven tightly, bright tomorrows.
Each emotion, a color, a hue,
In this tapestry, me and you.

Vibrant reds of passion's flame,
Softened blues of grief's name.
In every weave, a story lies,
A journey captured under the skies.

Golden threads of laughter bright,
Silvery strands in the calm of night.
Linked together, we find our way,
In this tapestry, we choose to stay.

From the loom of time, we spin and twist,
Every moment, a chance not missed.
In the pattern of life, we are one,
Through every season, through the sun.

As we gaze at the fabric, rich and true,
Each thread a moment shared by two.
In the tapestry, our hearts entwine,
In vivid colors, forever shine.

Echoes of Inner Harmony

In the stillness, the echoes rise,
Whispers of peace beneath the skies.
Melodies linger, soft and sweet,
In the heart's rhythm, we find our beat.

Harmony flows like a gentle stream,
Unveiling truths, igniting a dream.
With each note, the spirit sings,
In the silence, our freedom springs.

In every heartbeat, a world unfolds,
Stories of courage, brave and bold.
Echoes of laughter dance in the night,
Guided by love, we take flight.

Through every storm, we find our way,
In the echoes, we learn to stay.
With open hearts, we embrace the sound,
In inner harmony, we are bound.

As dawn approaches, light breaks anew,
Echoes of hope, steadfast and true.
In this symphony, we find our spark,
Together we journey, igniting the dark.

Reflections of Genuine Connections

In still waters, truth resides,
Faces mirrored, hearts confide.
Laughter dances in the sky,
Bonds unbroken, soaring high.

Whispers shared in moonlit glow,
Tales of old, where feelings flow.
Through trials faced and joys amassed,
Love's embrace, forever cast.

Silent moments, hands entwined,
Trust and care in every line.
A tapestry, rich and bright,
Woven deep in endless light.

With every glance, a spark ignites,
Endless days, and starry nights.
Connection found in souls so free,
In this bond, we always be.

Through life's storms, we find our way,
In each other, bright as day.
These reflections, pure and true,
Forever, I connect with you.

Seams of Sensitivity

In whispered tones, a soft embrace,
A gentle touch, a sacred space.
Feelings rise, like tides at sea,
In every heart, a symphony.

Threads of kindness weave the air,
Compassion found, we choose to care.
With open hearts, we dare to see,
The world beyond, you and me.

Emotions flow like rivers wide,
In every tear, there's hope inside.
With fragile hands, we mend the seams,
Creating trust, igniting dreams.

Softly spoken, truths arise,
In every word, no need for lies.
Sensitivity's the key, my friend,
In this journey, we transcend.

Together we can build a bridge,
Over valleys, through every ridge.
In unity, we find our song,
In seams of sensitivity, we belong.

Intertwined Hearts

In a garden where hope is sown,
Two hearts, as one, have brightly grown.
Hand in hand, through thick and thin,
In every loss, together we win.

Moonlit nights and sunny rays,
Intertwined in endless ways.
A language shared without a word,
In silence, love is truly heard.

With every beat, a sacred dance,
In harmony, a perfect chance.
Roots that twist beneath the earth,
In this bond, we find our worth.

Together we face what life imparts,
Through storms and calm, intertwined hearts.
In every challenge, we will find,
A deeper love that's intertwined.

With eyes that speak and smiles that spark,
In this journey, we leave our mark.
In the tapestry of life, so grand,
Our intertwined hearts forever stand.

Echoes of Empathic Understanding

In quiet moments, wisdom speaks,
An echo of the heart that seeks.
To understand, we listen deep,
In shared silence, secrets keep.

Through every story, pain is known,
Together, seeds of grace are sewn.
A gentle voice, a knowing glance,
In this dance, we find the chance.

With open arms, we learn to share,
The weight of burdens, the depth of care.
Echoes linger, soft and clear,
In understanding, we draw near.

The tapestry of life unfolds,
In every thread, a tale retold.
Compassion flows like rivers wide,
In each other, hope abides.

With empathy, our souls ignite,
Bringing shadows into light.
Together we rise, together we stand,
In echoes of understanding, hand in hand.

Bridges of Belonging

In the quiet dusk, we meet,
Hearts warm, no retreat.
Laughter echoes on the street,
Dancing souls in rhythmic beat.

Whispers shared under the stars,
Stories told of distant bars.
Every tale a guiding light,
Binding us through day and night.

Hands entwined, we walk as one,
Chasing dreams, fearing none.
In this space, we feel at home,
Together, never alone.

Footsteps traced on paths we know,
With every challenge, we grow.
Bridges built, both strong and wide,
In our hearts, love won't subside.

Through the storms, we find our peace,
In connection, doubts release.
Voices rise in harmony,
Creating bonds, eternally.

Each moment adds a brick anew,
Crafting ties that feel so true.
In this bond, our spirits sing,
Together, we can conquer anything.

Tales Weaving Together

Underneath the woven sky,
Stories blend, time rushes by.
Fragments lost, yet never broke,
In every word, a shared cloak.

Seasons change, but we remain,
In the laughter, in the pain.
Threads of lives intertwined,
In every heart, a tale aligned.

Echoes of the past resound,
In our souls, the truths are found.
Weaving dreams with vibrant hue,
Tales unfold as we renew.

Every moment, a stitch in time,
Crafting beauty in each rhyme.
Through the canvas, colors blaze,
Guiding us through life's maze.

In the tapestry we create,
Bound by love, we elevate.
In unity, our strength portrayed,
Stories shine, never fade.

Together we stand, side by side,
Woven tales our hearts abide.
In every whisper, every cheer,
A legacy we'll hold dear.

Portals of Passionate Exchange

In the realm where thoughts collide,
Ideas bloom, no need to hide.
Words like rivers, flowing free,
Each exchange a discovery.

Hearts laid bare in open space,
Finding strength in every face.
Embers glow within the night,
Passions rise, our shared delight.

Echoed voices intertwine,
In this dance, our paths align.
What we share creates the spark,
Lighting up the deepest dark.

Through these portals, doors we find,
Transforming souls, hearts combined.
Emotional bridges come alive,
In this realm, we truly thrive.

Every glance, a story told,
In each moment, hearts unfold.
Passionate exchange, a delight,
Fueling dreams that reach new heights.

Together we rise, hand in hand,
In these moments, we all stand.
Boundless love in every breath,
Fostering life that conquers death.

Shadows of Solidarity

In the quiet of the night,
Shadows dance, a hidden sight.
Silent vows among the trees,
Unity in every breeze.

Underneath the starlit sky,
Fears beside us, we defy.
Voices whispering in the dark,
In our hearts, they're leaving marks.

Every struggle faced as one,
Together, we will overcome.
Branches intertwined, we stand,
Holding tight, a promised hand.

Through the trials, we will rise,
In each tear, a strength supplies.
Shadows melt in morning light,
Showing paths that make us bright.

In this bond, we dare to dream,
Life's a choice, not just a scheme.
With our stories intertwined,
In each other, peace we find.

Shadows fade but spirits glow,
In solidarity, love flows.
Together we will always stay,
Chasing shadows far away.

Sails of Shared Journeys

In the dawn's embrace, we rise,
Sails unfurl beneath the skies.
Waves whisper tales of distant lands,
Together we steer with steady hands.

With every gust, our hearts entwine,
Navigating through the stormy brine.
The horizon glows, a beacon bright,
Guiding us home, a shared delight.

Memories echo in the sheening waves,
Each adventure, a story that paves.
Laughter dances on the ocean's breath,
In unity, we conquer even death.

As stars twinkle in the velvet night,
We chart our course, hearts taking flight.
Through tranquil seas and tempests fierce,
Our bonds grow strong, our dreams immerse.

When the journey ends, we look back,
Embracing the love that never lacks.
For every sail shared, every tide,
In our hearts, forever reside.

Merging Moods

Morning dew clings to the grass,
Whispers of light as moments pass.
Shades of gold blend with soft gray,
In the gentle light, emotions sway.

Amidst the chaos, a calm persists,
Balancing feelings in swirling mists.
Melodies weave, a vibrant thread,
Connecting souls where thoughts are spread.

Colors clash like voices raised,
In the heart's gallery, art is phrased.
Joy and sorrow, a canvas bright,
Held in the balance of day and night.

Underneath the ever-changing sky,
We find our place, we learn to fly.
Like rivers merging, we become whole,
Flowing freely, blending soul to soul.

In every heartbeat, a rhythm beats,
A testament to how love repeats.
Together we dance in the ambient sound,
In every mood, our truth is found.

Emotions in Confluence

Rivers meet where the currents blend,
Feelings flow, no need to pretend.
In the quiet, truths are laid bare,
Emotions intertwine in the air.

Softly the winds carry our sighs,
In the depth of gaze, a thousand ties.
With every heartbeat, the world aligns,
In the tapestry of love, our design.

Fading shadows as day unfolds,
Stories of courage waiting to be told.
With every step, we forge ahead,
In the light of trust where fears are shed.

In the confluence where dreams collide,
We find the strength that must abide.
Hand in hand, through tempests we tread,
Energized by the words unsaid.

Together we stand, both fierce and free,
In every embrace, a symphony.
In the waves of emotion, we dive deep,
Planting seeds of love, for us to keep.

Recollections of Resilience

In shadows cast, we find our light,
Memories of struggle igniting the fight.
Through woven tales of heart and stone,
We gather strength when we're all alone.

The scars we bear tell stories bold,
Of battles fought amidst the cold.
With every tear that stains the ground,
A testament to the strength we've found.

In laughter shared, we lift the weight,
Healing blooms where hope can penetrate.
Resilient hearts, like mountains stand,
Facing the world, hand in hand.

As seasons shift and years go by,
We carry on, learning to fly.
In the garden of time, we plant our seeds,
Nurturing dreams born from our needs.

Unyielding spirit, we rise anew,
In every sunrise, the chance to pursue.
Together we'll forge a brighter way,
Recollections of strength that forever stay.

Echoes of Empathy

In shadows deep, our hearts align,
A whispered thought, a rope to bind.
In silence shared, our worries fade,
The echoes speak, the fears allayed.

A light so soft, a gentle touch,
In moments small, we mean so much.
Together we rise, we weather storms,
With care and love, our spirit warms.

Through laughter bright and tears that fall,
We find our strength, we stand tall.
Empathy flows, a river wide,
In each heartbeat, a trusted guide.

A bridge we build, with words unspoken,
In every promise, a bond that's woven.
In listening hearts, we craft the way,
Through shared paths, come what may.

In peace we stand, in truth we speak,
Embracing difference, making us meek.
For in our souls, we're all the same,
Empathy's fire, an eternal flame.

Kaleidoscope of Connection

A prism bright, reflecting light,
In varied hues, our hearts take flight.
Through laughter's echo and sorrow's song,
In every color, we all belong.

The threads we weave, a tapestry bold,
Stories shared, in moments told.
Connections spark like stars at night,
Guiding us forth, in shared delight.

In every glance, a world we find,
United souls, our hearts entwined.
With open hands, we lift each other,
In every bond, we see a brother.

A mosaic made, from shards of light,
In all our differences, we shine bright.
With every touch, with every smile,
The beauty blooms, stretching a mile.

In harmony's dance, together we sway,
Finding the rhythm in the play.
Embracing change, we journey on,
A kaleidoscope where love is drawn.

Inner Landscapes United

Within the heart, vast realms reside,
A tranquil space where dreams abide.
Through mountain highs and valleys low,
In each heartbeat, our spirits grow.

The path we walk, though paved with strife,
Leads us to the core of life.
Through storms we march, side by side,
In unity's strength, our fears subside.

In quiet moments, wisdom speaks,
Each whisper know, a promise seeks.
We paint our journeys, brushstrokes bold,
In this vast land, our stories told.

With every tear, a seed is sown,
In every joy, a love is grown.
Together, navigating the unknown,
Our inner worlds, intertwined, alone.

With compassion's light, we guide the way,
In every heart, a brighter day.
Together we build, with hope anew,
Inner landscapes united, me and you.

Celestial Currents of Care

In cosmic dance, the stars align,
With every glance, your soul is mine.
In gentle sways, we find our truth,
Dreams intertwine, revealing youth.

Through tides of time, our spirits soar,
In currents bold, we yearn for more.
With every pulse, a bond that's shared,
In silence known, we've truly cared.

The moonlight's glow, a tender guide,
In every heartbeat, love's inter tide.
As constellations beckon our fate,
Across the vast, we navigate.

In whispers soft, the heavens sing,
Reminding us of the joy we bring.
Through trials faced, and dreams we chase,
In celestial waves, we find our place.

In unity's embrace, we drift away,
Carried by love, come what may.
In cosmic threads, our souls repair,
In celestial currents of endless care.

Flows of Fondness

In the river of time, moments drift,
Hearts intertwine, bonds softly shift.
Gentle whispers beneath the moonlight,
Filling the void, making all things right.

Laughter echoes in the warm breeze,
Memories woven like the rustling leaves.
Each glance, a chapter, each hug, a line,
In the book of us, forever entwined.

Through valleys low and mountains high,
We navigate the sky, you and I.
With every heartbeat, love finds its way,
Guiding us gently through each new day.

In the tapestry of what we share,
Threads of joy stitched with utmost care.
A canvas painted with colors bright,
Illuminate shadows, turn dark to light.

So here's to the flows, the endless streams,
To the dreams we build, to the laughter beams.
With fondness as our guiding star,
We'll dance together, no matter how far.

Stitches of Shared Smiles

In the fabric of life, smiles we sew,
Each thread a story, each laugh a glow.
Stitches of joy on a winter's day,
Binding our hearts in a playful sway.

Candles flicker, casting a warm light,
Shadows of memories taking flight.
Together we wander through fields of gold,
Shared smiles, a treasure, a delight to hold.

Through the storms, we stand side by side,
Each moment cherished, nothing to hide.
A quilt of kindness with colors so bright,
Stitched with love, a beautiful sight.

When days grow heavy, and shadows creep,
Our smiles can linger, our laughter sweep.
With every thread, our bond becomes tight,
In the warmth of shared moments, pure delight.

So raise your glass to the smiles we've shared,
To the laughter that dances, the moments cared.
With every stitch in this fabric fine,
We weave a life, forever entwined.

Resonance of Reciprocity

In the echoing halls of give and take,
We find our rhythm in each step we make.
A balance of kindness, a dance so sweet,
Two hearts in sync, a joyous heartbeat.

When you lift me up, I rise with grace,
In your love's warmth, I find my place.
Each gesture returned in a beautiful flow,
A cycle of love that wonders and grows.

Through trials faced and joys acclaimed,
In every moment, we remain untamed.
The whispers of trust in soft serenades,
Marking the path through life's cool glades.

So hand in hand, we'll journey on,
With reciprocity flowing like a song.
In this harmony, our spirits align,
Together we shine, as stars that entwine.

With open hearts, we'll always find,
A resonance sweet, soothing and kind.
In the dance of give and take, let's glide,
For in this balance, love shall abide.

Joys of Joint Journeys

Together we embark on paths unknown,
Through valleys deep, our courage has grown.
With every step, new horizons in sight,
Hand in hand, we chase the fading light.

Moments unfold like petals of spring,
In laughter and love, our hearts take wing.
Through every twist, through every turn,
In the flame of our bond, bright passions burn.

With dreams as our compass, we forge ahead,
In the tapestry of life, brightly thread.
Every memory stirs a sweet refrain,
In the joys of journeys, we find no pain.

Through sunsets kaleidoscope and dawn's first ray,
With shared adventures, we'll greet the day.
In the book of life, we're writing a tale,
A saga of hope, love's vibrant sail.

So here's to the travels, both near and far,
To dreams painted by our guiding star.
In the joys of joint journeys, we'll discover,
A world shaped by the love we uncover.

Collective Whisper of Souls

In the quiet night, thoughts align,
Voices blend softly, a sacred sign.
Stars twinkle gently, hearts in flight,
Together we wander, guided by light.

Shared dreams cradled in careful arms,
Echoes of laughter, timeless charms.
Winds carry stories, whispers of old,
In the tapestry spun, each thread is gold.

Paths intertwine, like roots of a tree,
In the garden of souls, we grow, we're free.
Hands clasped in unity, spirits embraced,
Together we flourish, in love interlaced.

When shadows may linger, and doubts arise,
We find strength together, in shared skies.
With every heartbeat, connections unfurl,
A symphony sweet in our wondrous swirl.

As the dawn approaches, we rise, we soar,
In the whisper of souls, we're forevermore.
Harmony found in the sacred blend,
Through love and whispers, our hearts transcends.

Resonance of Resilience

In the storms of life, we find our might,
Through trials we gather, igniting the light.
Each setback a chance, each tear a gain,
For in our reflections, we grow through pain.

With calloused hands, we build anew,
Brick by brick, with hope in view.
Every challenge a step, every fall a rise,
The fire within us, forever never dies.

Together we stand, a fortress of sparks,
Echoes of courage in the deepest dark.
Whispers of strength for those who roam,
In the heartbeat of unity, we find our home.

Through trials we march, undeterred and bold,
Chasing our dreams, breaking the mold.
For the spirit of resilience flows through our veins,
In the rhythm of struggle, our freedom reigns.

With voices united, we sing out loud,
In the face of despair, together we're proud.
For in every struggle, in each little fight,
Resilience blossoms and guides us to light.

Heartfelt Intertwining

Two hearts collide in the still of the night,
A dance of connection, pure and bright.
Soft words exchanged, like a gentle stream,
In the fabric of time, we weave our dream.

Eyes meet like rivers, flowing so deep,
In the garden of whispers, secrets we keep.
Fingers entwined, a promise so true,
In the warmth of our closeness, love's tender hue.

Each heartbeat a rhythm, a song of our own,
In the silence, our essence is beautifully shown.
With laughter like music, and tears like rain,
In the tapestry woven, we find peace in pain.

Days pass like pages in a book written slow,
In the laughter of seasons, together we grow.
Through mornings and twilight, hand in hand,
In the depths of our souls, forever we stand.

With whispers of kindness, we nurture our flame,
In the space of our love, we never feel shame.
With hearts interwoven, we shine and we glow,
In the bond of affection, endlessly flow.

Convergence of Kindred Spirits

In the embrace of dusk, kindred souls meet,
With laughter and stories, life feels complete.
Around the warm fire, connections ignite,
In the presence of friend, the world feels right.

Different paths traveled, yet hearts align,
In the dance of our spirits, we gently entwine.
With open arms, we gather and share,
In the tapestry woven, a bond beyond compare.

The air thick with dreams, hopes held so dear,
In the sanctuary found, there's nothing to fear.
With every heartbeat, a rhythm so sweet,
In the convergence of souls, our joys repeat.

Through laughter and tears, together we stand,
In the language of love, a gentle command.
With each moment lived, in truth we confide,
In the warmth of our circle, we cannot divide.

As the stars look down, we stand side by side,
In the glow of our spirits, there's nothing to hide.
Every whisper shared, every glance that lingers,
In the convergence of souls, forever, love simmers.

Harmony of the Soul

In whispers soft, where dreams unite,
The melody of hearts takes flight.
Within the silence, love finds its way,
Creating peace in the light of day.

A dance of shadows, a glow of grace,
Every heartbeat finds its place.
Through the chaos, we learn to sing,
Embracing joy that harmony brings.

The stars align in a cosmic embrace,
Guiding us through time and space.
In every sigh, a sacred tune,
Crafting a world beneath the moon.

In laughter shared, in sorrow's ache,
The threads of solace we gently make.
Together we rise, together we fall,
In harmony, we answer the call.

So let us weave this vibrant thread,
With every word that remains unsaid.
In the chorus of life, we find our role,
Creating the true harmony of the soul.

Confluence of Hearts

Two rivers flow, merging with grace,
In the tapestry of love, we find our place.
With every glance, a story unfolds,
In the warmth of connection, the heart beholds.

Hands entwined beneath the stars,
Carving memories that leave no scars.
Through whispered dreams and soft embraces,
In the confluence, time gently traces.

A language shared in silent glances,
In the heartbeat, our spirit dances.
Through shadows cast, through valleys deep,
These bonds we nurture, forever to keep.

When storms arise, we stand as one,
In unity, our battles are won.
Through trials faced, we bloom anew,
In the confluence, strength shines through.

So let us cherish this sacred start,
In the tapestry of life, we play our part.
With love's embrace, we rise above,
Together we thrive in the confluence of hearts.

Bonds Beyond Borders

Across the miles, our spirits meet,
In every heartbeat, love feels complete.
Bridges built from kindness and trust,
In a world united, we rise from dust.

Through valleys wide and mountains tall,
Our voices echo, answering the call.
No borders can break this joyful thread,
In the harmony of life, hope is bred.

In every language, a shared refrain,
Together we dance through joy and pain.
For in this journey, hand in hand,
We weave the fabric of a world so grand.

From distant shores to familiar lands,
In the bonds we nurture, hope expands.
Together we rise against the tide,
In bonds beyond borders, love will guide.

So let us celebrate this sacred quest,
Where every heart beats in its own jest.
In unity, the world we explore,
These bonds beyond borders, forevermore.

Threads of Human Experience

In the tapestry of time we weave,
Each moment shared, a gift to believe.
Through joys and sorrows, laughter and tears,
The threads of life connect our years.

With every heartbeat, stories unfold,
In the warmth of memories, we are bold.
From cherished times to lessons learned,\nIn this journey love is earned.

Through trials faced and mountains climbed,\nIn the echoing silence, we find what's primed.
Together we bloom, together we fade,
In the threads of being, foundations are laid.

In shared experience, wisdom grows,
In every challenge, the spirit knows.
Connecting us all in purpose clear,
Threads of human experience, held so dear.

So let us celebrate this grand design,
In every heart, a sacred line.
For in our stories, a truth so vast,
The threads of human experience will everlast.

Harmony in Hues

In the sun's warm embrace, we find grace,
Colors dance, each a joyful trace.
Whispers of pink and shades of blue,
Nature's palette in every view.

Soft greens laugh in the gentle breeze,
Yellows shimmer like honeyed trees.
Together they sing, bold and bright,
Creating a canvas, pure delight.

Clouds drift softly, a cotton dream,
Reflecting a world of vibrant theme.
In this beauty, we take our stand,
Connected deeply, hand in hand.

Crimson sunsets, where day meets night,
Each moment ignites our hearts with light.
In harmony's embrace, we shall roam,
Finding in colors, a sense of home.

With every hue, let spirits soar,
In this symphony, we want for more.
For in the blend, we truly see,
The endless beauty of you and me.

Refrain of Relatable Thoughts

In quiet corners of the mind,
Whispers of truth are intertwined.
Shared laughter, a familiar sound,
In each heart, a bond is found.

Glimpses of life, both joy and pain,
In every story, love's refrain.
With every doubt, a friend appears,
To hold us close and dry our tears.

Nightfall brings a soothing grace,
As stars align in endless space.
Conversations weave through the night,
As souls connect beneath soft light.

Echoes of dreams, honest and true,
Reminding us of what we knew.
With every heart, a common thread,
In shared moments, our spirits are fed.

In silence, a glance can speak more,
Binding us close, forever to explore.
In the rhythm of life, we find our way,
In relatable thoughts that softly stay.

Currents of Commonality

Rivers flow through every land,
Uniting souls with nature's hand.
A simple smile, a knowing glance,
In the current, we find our chance.

Through laughter shared and burdens light,
Together we stand, facing the night.
Each wave and tide tells stories old,
In unity, our hearts unfold.

Winds carry whispers along the shore,
Reminding us of what's in store.
In the ebb and flow, we rise and fall,
Connected deep, we hear the call.

Seas of dreams stretch far and wide,
On this journey, we'll take the ride.
For in our hearts, we share the light,
In currents strong, we'll find our sight.

A tapestry woven with threads so fine,
In the fabric of life, our souls align.
Through common waters, we shall sail,
Finding in each other, a shared tale.

Garden of Gentle Gestures

In gardens where the wildflowers bloom,
Soft petals greet the afternoon.
A tender touch, a warm embrace,
In gentle gestures, we find our place.

The rustling leaves speak secrets low,
Inviting us to let love grow.
With every seed, we plant our dreams,
Nurtured by the sunlight's beams.

A smile is sown, a kind word shared,
In every heart, compassion is spared.
In this garden, we learn to care,
Finding beauty in what we share.

Raindrops fall like joyful tears,
Washing away all doubts and fears.
In gentle rains, our spirits rise,
Underneath those vast, open skies.

As blossoms flourish, so do we,
In this haven, we're wild and free.
Through every gesture, small yet grand,
Together we cultivate, hand in hand.

The Language of Togetherness

In whispers soft, we share our dreams,
Laughter flows like gentle streams.
Hands entwined, we walk as one,
In unity, our hearts have spun.

With every glance, a silent song,
In this space, we all belong.
Words unspoken, bonds unmade,
Together in the light and shade.

Through trials faced, we rise and stand,
A tapestry woven hand in hand.
In every story, a truth we seek,
In every moment, together we speak.

The world may change, but we remain,
In joy and sorrow, love's refrain.
A quiet strength in the heart's embrace,
Together we find our rightful place.

So here we gather, souls aligned,
In the language of love, unconfined.
For in each other, we truly see,
The beauty of our unity.

Heartbeat of Humanity

In every breath, a pulse we share,
A rhythm felt everywhere.
With every heartbeat, echoes soar,
A symphony that we explore.

Through laughter bright, through tears we shed,
In this life, we forge ahead.
The bond of kin, the ties so strong,
Together we find where we belong.

In kindness shown, a gentle grace,
In simple acts, we find our place.
One heartbeat speaks to every soul,
In humanity, we are whole.

The pain of others, we can feel,
In sharing loss, we start to heal.
With open hearts, we bridge the gap,
In togetherness, we close the map.

So let us dance to love's sweet tune,
Under the sun, beneath the moon.
For every heartbeat tells a tale,
In harmony, we will not fail.

The Warmth of Shared Moments

In twilight glow, we gather near,
Shared moments wrap us, warm and clear.
With every smile, with every sigh,
In this embrace, we learn to fly.

Through cups of tea and stories spun,
The warmth we share has just begun.
In fleeting time, we find our peace,
A sanctuary that won't cease.

The laughter rises, the silence deep,
In these moments, memories keep.
A touch, a glance, a knowing nod,
In every heartbeat, love is prod.

Through seasons' change, we stand as one,
In summer's heat, in winter's fun.
Each shared moment, a thread we weave,
In this tapestry, we believe.

So let us cherish, hold it tight,
The warmth we find in every night.
For in these moments, life is sweet,
Together, our joy is complete.

Pathways of Understanding

On winding roads, we seek to know,
In every step, the seeds we sow.
With open minds and hearts to share,
On pathways lit, we find our care.

Through dialogues that bridge the gap,
We listen close, we fill the map.
In every story, lessons grow,
In understanding, futures flow.

Each journey taken, a step to learn,
In kindness shown, we brightly burn.
With empathy, we find our way,
Building pathways day by day.

The world unfolds, diverse and wide,
In every culture, love and pride.
Through shared experiences, we rise,
In unity, we see the skies.

So let us walk on this bright land,
In understanding, hand in hand.
For on this path, together we roam,
Creating a world, our shared home.

Navigating the Nexus of Hearts

In twilight's glow, we share a dream,
Waves of whispers, like a quiet stream.
Each heartbeat dances, a gentle sway,
Guiding our souls along the way.

Through tangled paths, we find our light,
Stars align in the velvet night.
With every step, we forge a bond,
In the stillness, our spirit's fond.

The nexus calls, a sacred space,
Where time is lost, and we embrace.
Two hearts beat in a rhythmic tune,
Under the watchful, silver moon.

In laughter's echo, joy unfolds,
A tapestry of warmth that holds.
In silent moments, we understand,
Navigating this heart-bound land.

Together we chart, uncharted seas,
With each soft breeze, our hearts at ease.
In this lovely dance, we take a part,
Navigating the nexus of hearts.

Tides of Togetherness

Amidst the waves, we find our shore,
Each tide a promise, forevermore.
With every ebb, our spirits rise,
In the moon's reflection, love complies.

We hold the sands, so fine, so true,
Cradling memories like morning dew.
In the rhythm of the ocean's call,
Together we stand, together we fall.

An endless dance, the water swirls,
Embracing dreams as time unfurls.
With hearts as anchors, strong and deep,
We sail this journey, never to weep.

Along the shoreline, hand in hand,
In whispers soft, we understand.
Our love, a lighthouse, guiding near,
Through misty mornings, we persevere.

With every sunset, colors blend,
A masterpiece that will not end.
In the tides of togetherness, we trust,
Forever entwined, it's a must.

Confluence of Connections

In the stillness, our voices blend,
Threads of fate that gently send.
Winding rivers, where we meet,
At the confluence, our hearts repeat.

With open arms, we share our dreams,
Like gentle currents, flowing streams.
In laughter, tears, we find the way,
Building bridges when skies are gray.

Whispers echo through the night,
In quiet moments, our souls ignite.
The world around us fades away,
In this confluence, we long to stay.

Our paths converge, a dance we share,
In every glance, a loving stare.
Together we rise, together we shine,
In this sacred space, so divine.

Forever marked by this sweet grace,
In every heartbeat, we find our place.
Through the confluence of connections true,
I am forever lost in you.

Alchemy of Affection

In hidden labs, we weave our spells,
With every glance, the magic swells.
An alchemy born from tender hearts,
Transforming moments into art.

With sweet elixirs, laughter brews,
In potions made from vibrant hues.
We mix our dreams, let colors fly,
Creating wonders that could never die.

In sacred silence, we find the keys,
Unlocking secrets with gentle ease.
The alchemists of love we stand,
Crafting a world, hand in hand.

In every heartbeat, sparks ignite,
Fusing our souls in radiant light.
This alchemy, a treasured song,
In each embrace, we both belong.

Forever bound by this sweet potion,
Dancing through life with pure devotion.
In the alchemy of affection's play,
We write our love in endless way.

Symphony of Sentiments

In the silence of night, whispers play,
Melodies of hearts in a gentle sway.
Notes of laughter, shadows of sorrow,
A tune of today, a hope for tomorrow.

Each heartbeat echoes in soft refrain,
Binding our souls in joy and in pain.
Like a hidden song that stirs deep within,
Awakening dreams where love can begin.

Through the chaos, we find our rhyme,
In the dance of the stars, we're lost in time.
Together we spin in this cosmic dance,
Finding our way in a fleeting glance.

The symphony rises, a powerful tide,
Carving our path, with courage as guide.
In the harmony woven, hearts beat as one,
A chorus of life under the sun.

So let the sounds of our spirits combine,
Creating a world where love will shine.
In the symphony's embrace, we shall reside,
Together in music, with arms open wide.

Embrace of Emotions

In the warmth of the sun, moments entwine,
Feelings like flowers in the softest align.
Each petal a heartbeat, each stem a sigh,
In the garden of hope, we learn to fly.

With every glance, a story unfolds,
With laughter and tears, our truth is told.
The tapestry rich with colors so bold,
In the embrace of emotions, we break the mold.

Through the storms that may come, we stand side by side

Navigating life with love as our guide.
In the ocean of feelings, we dive and we swim,
With hearts wide open, our spirits brim.

Here in the stillness, we dare to be real,
Sharing the depths, an unspoken seal.
In the embrace of emotions, we find our place,
Wrapped tightly in warmth, in love's sweet grace.

So rise with the dawn, let your heart be free,
In the poetry of life, just you and me.
We'll cherish the moments, the highs and the lows,
In the embrace of emotions, together we grow.

Tapestry of Heartstrings

In the loom of existence, threads intertwine,
Creating a tapestry both fragile and fine.
Each heart a strand, woven with care,
Bound by the love that we gladly share.

The colors of joy blend with shades of pain,
A portrait of life, a dance in the rain.
With each stitch, we gather and weave,
Stories of hope that we won't leave.

In moments of silence, our hearts can speak,
Finding the strength in the soft and weak.
As shadows may linger, light softly grows,
In the tapestry woven, our true essence glows.

Beneath the vast sky, we embrace the night,
Dreaming our dreams in the soft moonlight.
With hands intertwined, we face what's ahead,
In the tapestry of heartstrings, we're lovingly led.

So gather the threads, let's create a design,
A colorful journey, your heart next to mine.
In the art of our love, forever we'll stay,
In the tapestry of heartstrings, come what may.

Unity in Vulnerability

In the softness of truth, we dare to unfold,
Revealing our hearts, stories untold.
With courage as armor, we stand tall and bare,
In the unity found when we choose to share.

Like petals that open in the warmest embrace,
Vulnerability brings us to a sacred space.
Here, we find strength in being sincere,
In the beauty of flaws, our hearts hold dear.

Amidst the chaos, we gather as one,
Finding the light when the day is done.
With voices in harmony, fears set aside,
In unity's grasp, we boldly reside.

In the depths of connection, our spirits align,
Crafting a bond that is pure and divine.
Each whisper, each shadow, we lovingly claim,
In the unity of vulnerability, we're not the same.

So let us embrace all we have inside,
In the sea of emotions, we will not hide.
Together as one, we can learn to be free,
In the unity of vulnerability, just you and me.

Seeds of Sincere Connection

In silent glances, bonds are sown,
A shared laugh, a moment grown,
Roots deepen in the soil of trust,
Together, rise, it's a must.

Through storms that test, we learn to stand,
With open hearts, we hold the hand,
Each word a seed, each story shared,
In truth's embrace, we are prepared.

Patience nurtures what's begun,
In shared silence, two become one,
With every tear, a flower blooms,
In friendship's light, dispel the glooms.

Laughter echoes through the years,
Through joy and sorrow, shared tears,
In every sigh, in every cheer,
We plant the seeds of love sincere.

And as we grow, our branches wide,
In unity, we both abide,
With roots entwined, a sturdy lace,
In this garden, we find our place.

Radiance of Resilient Relationships

In the glow of caring eyes,
We rise again, we touch the skies,
Through trials faced, we find our light,
In unity, we shine so bright.

Each challenge faced, a lesson learned,
In every heart, a fire burned,
With whispered hopes and dreams held tight,
Our spirits soar into the night.

Through shifting sands and winds that blow,
Together strong, we choose to grow,
A tapestry of shared delight,
In every moment, we unite.

And when the shadows start to creep,
In laughter's arms, our joy runs deep,
In bonds of hope, we find our way,
Each dawn, a gift, a brand new day.

In gentle strength, we hold each other,
Through every storm, we are no other,
In radiant hearts, our truth revealed,
Resilient love, forever sealed.

Colors of Communal Care

In vibrant hues, our spirits blend,
A canvas bright where hearts extend,
With every stroke, a story shared,
In colors bold, our love declared.

Through laughter's ring and tender voices,
Together we make joyful choices,
In every shade, a memory shines,
In community, our light defines.

With open arms, we greet the day,
In unity, we choose to play,
Our differences, a rich delight,
In every heart, a spark of light.

In hugs that warm, and words that heal,
We paint a truth that is all real,
Through kindness shared, we build anew,
In colors bright, we see our view.

Together, woven, hearts sincere,
In every moment, we draw near,
In the art of care, we find our flair,
A masterpiece, this love we share.

Canopy of Companionship

Underneath the sturdy trees,
In whispered winds, a gentle breeze,
Together, sheltered from the storm,
In friendship's shade, we find our form.

With branches strong, we reach so high,
In laughter's lift, we learn to fly,
Through seasons change, roots intertwine,
In every heart, our love aligns.

In moments quiet, we find peace,
In shared breaths, our worries cease,
Through open skies and morning light,
In this embrace, we hold on tight.

When shadows fall, we stand as one,
In every challenge, we have won,
In loyalty's knot, we find our way,
A canopy that will not sway.

Through twilight gleams and dawn's new spark,
We share our dreams, ignite the dark,
In companionship, we find our grace,
Together here, we've found our place.

Web of Warmth

A thread connects each heart,
In laughter and in tears.
Wrapped in a gentle glow,
We cast aside our fears.

Through storms that come our way,
We hold each other tight.
In shadows brightened forth,
We find our strength in light.

The bonds we weave are strong,
With love that knows no end.
In moments of sweet grace,
We cherish and we mend.

From branches intertwined,
A tapestry unfolds.
In every whispered dream,
The warmth of kinship holds.

Together we will stand,
Against the world we fight.
With hearts forever joined,
In this web, pure delight.

Kinship of Kindred Spirits

We gather like the stars,
In night's deep velvet hue.
Each soul a spark of joy,
A bond so pure and true.

Through laughter, tears, and tales,
In silence, we connect.
In shadows or in light,
Our hearts are intertwined.

The kinship lights our path,
In joy and sorrow shared.
Together we are whole,
In dreams, we are prepared.

With every step we take,
We write our destinies.
Kindred spirits entwined,
A dance through memories.

From whispered thoughts in dusk,
To dawn's soft golden plea,
We stand as one, alive,
In harmony, so free.

Mosaic of Maverick Minds

In colors bold and bright,
We paint a world anew.
With strokes of wild ideas,
And visions shining through.

A canvas full of dreams,
United by our craft.
Each piece a work of art,
A journey through the draft.

The spark of creativity,
In every heart resides.
With every twist and turn,
The innovation guides.

Together we break molds,
With courage in our hands.
Our stories intertwined,
A tapestry of plans.

In this mosaic bright,
We celebrate the strange.
Maverick minds unite,
In endless paths of change.

Unison in Uncertainty

In a world that sways and bends,
We find our steady ground.
With hearts aligned in trust,
Together we are found.

Through whispers of doubt cast,
We face the unknown fears.
In shadows of the night,
Our light will guide us here.

With every step we take,
In tandem, we will move.
The harmony we seek,
In connection, we will prove.

Embracing all the stress,
With unity our shield.
In unison we'll stand,
In faith, our fate is sealed.

So here's to pathways crossed,
In uncertainty we thrive.
With hope and hearts entwined,
Together, we survive.

Milton Keynes UK
Ingram Content Group UK Ltd.
UKHW022048111124
451035UK00014B/1005